God Feeds Us
Bible Story Magazine

Augsburg Fortress
Minneapolis

Contents

Jesus Feeds 5,000 (Mark 6:30-44) 3

Jacob and Esau (Genesis 27) 12

Manna in the Wilderness (Exodus 15:22—16:36) 21

Peter and Cornelius (Acts 10:1-48) 30

Elijah and the Widow (1 Kings 17) 38

"God Feeds Us" Bible Story Magazine
For Grades 5-6
By Kaylene Johnson

Each Bible story magazine has one one age-appropriate leader pack to accompany it.

Other series components available for Grades 5-6:
"God Feeds Us" Grades 5-6 Leader Pack
"God Feeds Us" Grades 1-6 Learning Tool
"God Feeds Us" Reproducible Home Pages

Editors: Cynthia Z. Biddlecomb and James Satter
Series Designer: Bozell Kamstra
Illustrators: Linda Rubietta/Bozell Kamstra (color illustrations);
    Chris Wold Dyrud and Brian Jensen (black-and-white illustrations)
Cover Photos: Digital Vision (front); © 2001 PhotoDisc, Inc.(back)

Scripture quotations marked CEV are from the Contemporary English Version text, copyright © 1991 American Bible Society. Used by permission.

Text, maps, and illustrations marked TLB are adapted from The Learning Bible © 2000, American Bible Society. Used by permission.

Copyright © 2001 Augsburg Fortress. All rights reserved. May not be reproduced.

ISBN 0-8066-6424-X

Manufactured in U.S.A.

1 2 3 4 5 6 7 8 9 0 1 2 3 4 5 6 7 8 9 0

Jesus Feeds 5,000

Mark 6:30-44

Hungry crowds gather around, wondering who this man Jesus is and what he will say next. Many of the people are healed. They all witness the ... MIRACLE OF 5,000.

Continued on page 4

Continued from page 3

After the apostles returned to Jesus, they told him everything they had done and taught. But so many people were coming and going that Jesus and the apostles did not even have a chance to eat. Jesus said, "Let's go to a place where we can be alone and get some rest." Jesus and the apostles left in a boat for a place where they could be alone. Many people saw them leave, however, and figured out where they were going. People from every town rushed on ahead and got there first. (verses 30-33, CEV)

Superstar!

Jesus said, "I am the bread that gives life!" Read what Jesus says about life-giving bread in John 6:35-40.

What would you do if some famous people came to your town? Would you want to see them? Get their autographs? Maybe talk to them in person?

Jesus became famous wherever he went. People followed him the way people today might follow a celebrity. But Jesus was not a famous actor, musician, or athlete; instead he healed people's bodies and spirits. Through his miracles and teachings, Jesus helped people to understand God's love and to love each other.

The crowds didn't realize that God had a plan beyond their wildest dreams. Through Jesus, God intended to rescue the world from sin. As the Son of God, Jesus would become the king of all and the ruler of our hearts.

Say What?

Jesus thought of people as sheep? It turns out that sheep and people aren't so different. Sheep need lots of attention and care. Sheep become familiar with the voice of their shepherd and follow when the shepherd calls. That's why Jesus called himself the "good shepherd." [TLB, p. 1830]

What Can I Give?

The disciples couldn't imagine what Jesus meant when he said to give the people something to eat. What did they have to offer?

Jesus had an important lesson to teach the disciples. When we give what we have—even though it may not seem like much—God blesses our offering and uses it to nourish others. God provides for need, but not for greed. (Read about what happened to people who took more food than they needed in Exodus 15:17-20.)

Can you think of ways that God might use you to nourish others, both in body and in spirit?

When Jesus got out of the boat, he saw a large crowd of people that was like a flock of sheep without a shepherd. Jesus felt sorry for the people and started to teach them many things.

That evening the disciples came to Jesus and said, "This place is like a desert, and it is already late. Let the crowds leave, so they can go to the farms and villages near here and buy something to eat."

Jesus replied, "You give them something to eat." (verses 34-37, CEV)

Continued on page 6

Continued from page 5

But they asked him, "Don't you know that it would take almost a year's wages to buy all of these people something to eat?"

Then Jesus said, "How much bread do you have? Go and see!" They found out and answered, "We have five small loaves of bread and two fish." (verses 37-38, CEV)

Try This

In Jesus' day, a year's wages were equal to about 200 silver coins. Each coin was the average day's wage for a worker.
(TLB, p. 1830)

Figure out how much it costs to buy a hamburger and french fries. Then multiply that amount times 5,000. That's how much money it would take to feed the crowd that had come to hear Jesus speak! What else could you buy for that amount of money? Look at the classified advertisements in a newspaper to see how much some jobs pay per hour or per year. How long would it take to earn enough to feed 5,000 people?

Key Verse

Jesus ... looked up toward heaven and blessed the food. Then he broke the bread and handed it to his disciples to give to the people. (Mark 6:41, CEV)

Jesus blessed the food . . . broke the bread: This same language is used when Jesus later shares a final meal with his disciples. (TLB, p.1831) **Read more in Mark 14:22-26.**

Jesus told his disciples to have the people sit down on the green grass. They sat down in groups of 100 and groups of 50.

Jesus took the five loaves and two fish, then looked up toward heaven and blessed the food. Then Jesus broke the bread and handed it to the disciples to give to the people. Jesus also divided the two fish, so that everyone could have some. (verses 39-41, CEV)

Continued on page 8

Continued from page 7

After everyone had eaten all they wanted, Jesus' disciples picked up 12 large baskets of leftover bread and the fish. There were 5,000 men who ate the food.

(verses 42-44, CEV)

I Was There!

Eyewitness Tells All!

I wasn't exactly thrilled about going to hear some guy talk. But my parents said we were going as a family, so that settled it. We walked a long way, and by the time we got there my little sister was complaining about being hungry. We all wished we had something to eat.

We sat near the front of the crowd and I overheard Jesus say to his disciples, "You feed them." They looked shocked and disbelieving. Then the disciples gathered a few loaves of bread and a couple of fish and brought the food to Jesus.

I know this is hard to believe, but I saw this with my own eyes. Jesus blessed the bread and broke it. Suddenly, out of nowhere, baskets were overflowing with fresh bread and fish! There was more than enough for everyone. Take it from me, this Jesus is powerful. I'm not sure what he'll do next, but I'll sure be watching!

For more exciting miracles, check out page 10!

Ask Abner

Dear Abner: I have plenty to eat, but still I feel kind of empty inside. I've been to the doctor and she says everything's OK. So, why do I feel restless and alone?—Worried

Dear Worried: First, let me assure you that you are NOT alone. People since the beginning of time have suffered from your ailment. What you have is heart-hunger. This is both bad news and good news. The bad news is we are all born with it—it started when sin entered the world. (See Genesis 3.) The good news is that there is a remedy for sin! Jesus fills the empty places we feel inside. By trusting in Jesus' love and forgiveness, our hearts are filled to overflowing. Instead of feeling so much loneliness, or anger, or sadness, we can feel peace. (Remember, Jesus said, "I am the bread that gives life!") So pray and trust God, and you will discover that joy in Jesus is contagious!

CAMPFIRE TALK

Jesus was a miracle worker, a healer, and a teacher. But who was he REALLY?

CLUES: *John 3:16-17; John 11:25-26; 1 John 5:20.*

Other Well-Known Miracles of Jesus

No wonder crowds gathered wherever Jesus went! He had the power to heal the sick. He could command the wind and waves. Jesus even brought people back to life! The chart below lists some well-known miracles of Jesus. Read the list and choose several to look up in your Bible. As you read the passages, imagine what it would have been like to witness these events. Imagine the sights and sounds and smells. How would you have felt?

Miracle	Scripture Passages
Turns water into wine in Cana.	John 2:1-11
Orders the wind and waves to be quiet.	Mark 4:35-41
Walks on water on Lake Galilee.	Matthew 14:22-33
Raises his friend Lazarus to life.	John 11:17-44
Raises a dead girl to life.	Matthew 9:18-26
Gives sight to a man born blind.	John 9:1-41
Cures the woman who had been bleeding for 12 years.	Matthew 9:20-22
Cures a man of evil spirits and sends the spirits into a herd of pigs.	Mark 5:1-20
Heals 10 men with leprosy.	Luke 17:11-19
Heals a disabled man in Capernaum.	Mark 2:1-12
Heals a man who was deaf.	Mark 7:31-37
Heals the high priest's servant after the man's ear is cut off.	Luke 22:49-52

[TLB, p. 1727]

SO WHO'S COUNTING?

Certain numbers had special meaning in the ancient world and to the writers of the Bible. The number 12 represented completeness and perfection. There were 12 baskets of food left over after Jesus fed 5,000 people. Here are more examples of the importance of 12.

- The number of Jacob's sons and the number of tribes of Israel (Genesis 35:23-26; 49:1-28)

- The number of gates to Jerusalem in Ezekiel's vision (Ezekiel 48:30; Revelation 21:11-21)

- The number of Jesus' apostles (Matthew 10:1-4; Mark 3:13-19; Luke 6:12-16; Acts 1:12-26)

[TLB, p. 2310]

Think about it: *How many inches are on a foot-long ruler? How many doughnuts are in a dozen? The importance of certain numbers in ancient times still has an impact on us today.*

Jacob and Esau

Genesis 27

Two brothers contend for a blessing and inheritance from their father. See what happens ... WHEN TWINS FIGHT.

After Isaac had become old and almost blind, he called in his firstborn son, Esau, who asked him, "Father, what can I do for you?"

Isaac replied, "I am old and might die at any time. So take your bow and arrows, then go out into the fields, and kill a wild animal. Cook some of that tasty food that I love so much and bring it to me. I want to eat it once more and give you my blessing before I die." (verses 1-4, CEV)

Continued on page 14

Powerful Stuff!

Spoken promises and deathbed blessings were important to many ancient people. (Read more about it in Genesis 48:8-20; 49:1-28; Deuteronomy 33; Joshua 23.) Such blessings were considered so powerful that they could not be taken back.

[TLB, p. 82]

Battle of the Brothers

Jacob and Esau were fighting even before they were born! The twins wrestled just to see who would be born first. Esau was born first, but Jacob was clutching Esau's heel as if to say, "Wait! I'm supposed to be first!"

Esau was covered with red hair when he was born. The name Esau sounds like the Hebrew word for "hairy."

The name Jacob sounds like the Hebrew word for "heel" or "he takes by the heel." The name Jacob also sounds like the Hebrew word for "cheat."

Eventually Esau forgave Jacob for cheating him out of his rights as Isaac's firstborn son. Read about how these long-embattled brothers finally found peace in Genesis 32–33.

Continued from page 13

Rebekah had been listening. As soon as Esau left to go hunting, Rebekah said to Jacob, "I heard your father tell Esau to kill a wild animal and cook some tasty food for your father before he dies. Your father said this because he wants to bless your brother with the Lord as his witness. Now, my son, listen carefully to what I want you to do. Go and kill two of your best young goats and bring them to me. I'll cook the tasty food that your father loves so much. Then you can take it to him, so he can eat it and give you his blessing before he dies." (verses 5-10, CEV)

"My brother Esau is a hairy man," Jacob reminded his mother. "And I am not. If my father touches me and realizes I am trying to trick him, he will put a curse on me instead of giving me a blessing."

(verses 11-12, CEV)

Rebecca Speaks Out

Listen, maybe you think I'm a deceitful person, but I had reasons for doing the things I did! (See Genesis 25:22-34.)

First, God practically told me that Jacob should receive Isaac's blessing. Before I gave birth to Jacob and Esau, I could feel them fighting with each other. I asked God about this and God said, "Your two sons will become separate nations. The younger of the two will be stronger and the older son will be his servant." So when Isaac told Esau he wanted to give him the blessing, I had to take matters into my own hands—to make sure Jacob received the blessing instead.

Second, Esau sold his birthright to Jacob a long time ago! One day, Esau came home from hunting and rudely demanded to eat the soup that Jacob was making. Jacob refused unless Esau first gave him his rights as the firstborn son. Esau agreed, so Jacob gave him some bread and soup. Later, Esau acted as though he'd never agreed to anything! Maybe I was dishonest by encouraging Jacob's trick. I thought I was doing the right thing, but now Esau is so angry. Only God can get us through this mess now.

—Rebekah

Rebekah insisted, "Let his curse fall on me! Just do what I say and bring me the meat." So Jacob brought the meat to his mother, and she cooked the tasty food that his father liked. Then she took Esau's best clothes and put them on Jacob. She also covered the smooth part of his hands and neck with goatskins and gave him some bread and the tasty food she had cooked. (verse 13-17, CEV)

Continued on page 16

Continued from page 15

Jacob went to his father and said, "Father, here I am." Then Isaac said, "Son, come over here and kiss me." While Jacob was kissing him, Isaac caught the smell of his clothes and said:

> The blessing Isaac gave to Jacob may not sound that great to us. But to people living off the land, the promise of abundant harvests truly was a blessing. What's more, Jacob is told that he will be the head of the family over his brother. It is Jacob's descendants, not Esau's, who will become the "12 tribes of Israel."

"The smell of my son is like a field the Lord has blessed. God will bless you, my son, with dew from heaven and with fertile fields, rich with grain and grapes. Nations will be your servants and bow down to you. You will rule over your brothers and they will kneel at your feet." (verses 18a, 26-29, CEV)

Key Verse

God will bless you ... with dew from heaven and with fertile fields, rich with grain and grapes. (Genesis 27:28, CEV)

TAKING AIM!

The spoken blessing was like an arrow shot at a target. Once it was released, it could not be taken back. Esau also wanted a blessing, but Isaac could not undo the blessing he had already given Jacob, which gave Jacob the right to rule over Esau. The blessing was to be the birthright of the firstborn, but Esau had already sold his birthright to Jacob.
(See Genesis 25:27-33.)
[TLB, p. 83]

Right after Isaac had given Jacob his blessing and Jacob had gone, Esau came back from hunting.... Esau cried loudly and begged, "Father, give me a blessing too!" (verses 30, 34, CEV)   Continued on page 18

Esau and his descendants (children born to his Hittite wives) later become a nation known as Edom. The Israelites had many disputes with their cousins the Edomites. (See Genesis 27:46.)

Isaac answered, "Your brother tricked me and stole your blessing."

Esau hated Jacob because he had stolen the blessing that was supposed to be his. So he said to himself, "Just as soon as my father dies, I'll kill Jacob."

When Rebecca found out what Esau planned to do, she sent for Jacob and told him, "Go to the home of my brother Laban in Haran and stay with him for a while. When Esau stops being angry and forgets what you have done to him, I'll send for you to come home."

(verses 35, 41-42a, 43b-45, CEV)

WANTED!

Second-born son of Isaac. Has smooth skin. Goes by the name of Jacob but may be using an alias. If you know of Jacob's whereabouts please contact me.

—*Esau*

Dear Abner: I'm so mad! Whether or not it's fair, my brother always seems to get his own way. I'm sick of it and want to get even. Do you have any ideas?—Seething

Dear Seething: I know how you feel—everyone has felt angry at one time or another. Sometimes the people we're supposed to love are the very people who anger us the most. Trying to get even isn't a good idea—all you'll do is start a family feud, and there are already enough of those to go around! For some good ideas about what to do, read Luke 6:31; James 1:19-20; Ephesians 4:26; 1 Peter 4:8. Then pray for God to guide you.

CAMPFIRE TALK

God's actions overrule human laws and customs. (See Romans 9:11-12.) No matter what we plan, or how we argue, or who we think is in charge, over time God's action in our lives becomes clear. In your own life, can you think of times when God worked through unusual events? [TLB, p. 79]

What's Up?
Why was "birthright" so important?

Israel and other parts of the ancient Near East gave special honor and privileges to the oldest son in every family. This "birthright" also included a special share in the family inheritance and leadership of the family after the father died (Deuteronomy 21:15-17). But these special rights could be transferred, as when Esau (the firstborn son of Isaac) sold his birthright to Jacob (Genesis 25:29-34).

In some cases, however, the notion of birthright was ignored and the oldest son was passed over or rejected. An example of this is the way God chose David, the youngest of Jesse's eight sons, to be the king of Israel (1 Samuel 16:1-13). God treated the whole people of Israel as God's firstborn offspring. In the Bible, God is described as being happy over this special relationship between them. Later, the prophet Jeremiah says that God rejoices when Israel (the disobedient child) returns and their close relationship is restored (Jeremiah 31:8-9).
[TLB, p.79]

So, what does this mean to me?

Through Jesus, we inherit the kingdom of God! Through baptism, we are like God's "firstborn," receiving the once-and-forever blessing of God's love and forgiveness.

Manna in the Wilderness

Exodus 15:22—16:36

The Israelites were freed from slavery in Egypt—only to find themselves facing the ultimate test of ... SURVIVAL!

Continued on page 22

Continued from page 21

There in the desert they started complaining to Moses and Aaron, saying, "We wish the Lord had killed us in Egypt. When we lived there we could at least sit down and eat all the bread and meat we wanted. But you have brought us out here into this desert, where we are going to starve."

The Lord said to Moses, "I will send bread down from heaven like rain. Each day the people can go out and gather only enough for that day. That's how I will see if they obey me. But on the sixth day of each week they must gather and cook twice as much."

Moses turned to Aaron and said, "Bring the people together, because the Lord has heard their complaints." (verses 2-5,9, CEV)

Now What? *After years of brutal slavery at the hands of Pharaoh, God delivered the Israelites in a dramatic rescue from Egypt. At first, people rejoiced in their freedom. But they found themselves in a wilderness where food was scarce and water was hard to come by. How would they survive?*

Quail are small, brown or sandy-colored birds that look similar to pheasants. Quail often migrate to the region of Palestine in large flocks during March or April. These birds usually fly low and prefer to run along the ground.
[TLB, p.161]

In Hebrew, the word ***manna*** means "What is it?" Manna was thin, like a wafer, and it could be baked or boiled.

Aaron was speaking to them, when everyone looked out toward the desert and saw the bright glory of the Lord in a cloud. The Lord said to Moses, "I have heard my people complain. Now tell them that each evening they will have meat and each morning they will have more than enough bread. Then they will know that I am the Lord their God."

That evening a lot of quail came and landed everywhere in the camp, and the next morning dew covered the ground. After the dew had gone, the desert was covered with thin flakes that looked like frost. The people had never seen anything like this, and they started asking each other, "What is it?" (verses 10-15a, CEV)

Continued on page 25

Moses, Man of God

Blaze goes behind the scenes to talk to Moses, a true person of God. Let's find out what he has to say about his adventures. (To read more about the story, look up the Bible passages mentioned in Moses' answers.)

Blaze: How did you become the leader of these people?

Moses: Believe me, at first, I didn't want the job. Eventually I was willing to do what God asked. So here I am. I'm glad that my brother Aaron is helping me (Exodus 3:1—4:17).

Blaze: What has been the hardest part of your job?

Moses: Without question, the hardest part is convincing people to trust God. You know how God parted the Red Sea for us to escape Egypt (Exodus 14). Time and time again, these people forget what God has done for us. Just the other day, some of them ignored God's instructions and took more manna than they needed. *(He laughs.)* The next day their extra manna was a stinking mess!

Blaze: Where are you and your people headed?

Moses: Ever since the time of Abraham, Isaac, and Jacob, God has promised us a land rich with milk and honey. Eventually God will lead us to the land of Canaan (Exodus 6:2-4). At the rate we're going, though, it could take a while.

Blaze: Do you have any advice for people trying to survive difficult times?

Moses: Yes! Trust in God. God really loves you!

Continued from page 23

Picking up bread (manna), quail, or grain on the Sabbath would have been considered work, so it was forbidden.

> For more about the Sabbath, read "Sabbath: A Weekly Festival" on page 28.

Moses answered, "This is the bread that the Lord has given you to eat. And he orders you to gather about two quarts for each person in your family—that should be more than enough."

They did as they were told. Some people gathered more and some gathered less, according to their needs, and none was left over.

Moses told them not to keep any overnight. Some of them disobeyed, but the next morning what they kept was stinking and full of worms, and Moses was angry. (verses 15b-20, CEV)

Continued on page 26

"GIVE US THIS DAY OUR DAILY BREAD"

Does that sound familiar? When Jesus gave the disciples these words to pray, they might have remembered the story of manna in the wilderness. Like the Israelites, we have to learn to trust that God gives enough for the needs of the world. If we only take as much as we need, nothing will go to waste. Find out about food-sharing programs in your area. What can you do to help?

Continued from page 25

Each morning everyone gathered as much food as they needed, and in the heat of the day the rest melted. However, on the sixth day of the week everyone gathered enough to have four quarts instead of two. The Lord had said, "Tomorrow is the Sabbath, a sacred day of rest in honor of me. So gather all you want to bake or boil and make sure you save enough for tomorrow."

The Israelites called the bread "manna." It was white like coriander seed and delicious as wafers made with honey.

Then Moses told Aaron, "Put some manna in a jar and store it in the place of worship for future generations to see." Aaron followed the Lord's instructions and put the manna in front of the sacred chest for safekeeping. (verses 21-23, 31, 33-34, CEV)

Key Verse

*"Then they will know that I am the L*ORD *their God." (Exodus 16:12, CEV)*

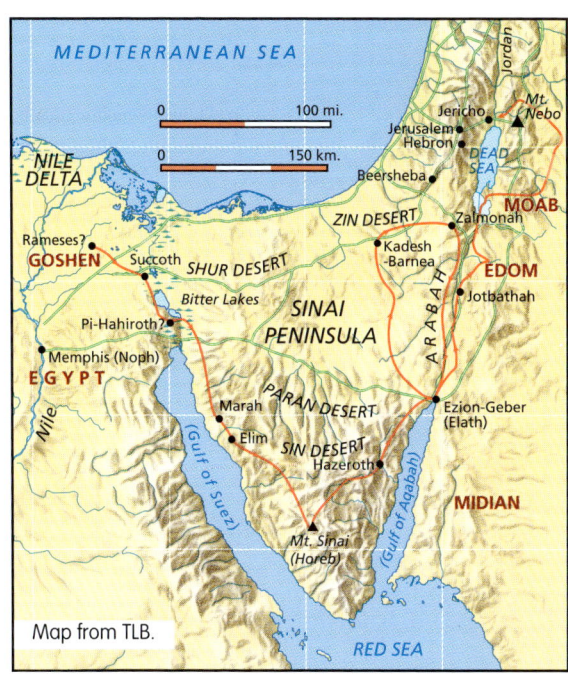

The Israelites wandered for 40 years in the desert before God led them to the promised land.

Find Marah.

Locate Mt. Sinai.

The Sacred Chest

A sacred chest, sometimes called the Ark of the Covenant, represented God's holy presence in the lives of people. Made of acacia wood and covered with gold, it contained the stone tablets of the Ten Commandments. It also contained a pot of manna and Aaron's rod. During their adventures in the wilderness, the Israelites kept the chest inside a sacred tent called a tabernacle. King Solomon eventually built a temple for the sacred chest. The temple was as beautiful as the sacred chest. The temple provided a permanent place to worship God and offer sacrifices for people's sins. [TLB, p. 505]

Illustration from TLB.

Sabbath
A Weekly Festival

The word *Sabbath* comes from the Hebrew verb *shahbat* (to "stop" or to "rest") and refers to the seventh day of the week, from sunset on Friday to sunset on Saturday. The ancient Israelites, like modern Jews, worshiped on the Sabbath and rested from their work.

The Sabbath's origin is found in Genesis 2:1-3. God rested from the work of creation on the seventh day and made it a special, holy day. In Exodus a connection is made between God's resting from creation and commanding Israel to rest from work on the Sabbath and worship the Lord (Exodus 20:8-11; 31:17). This resting was not only for the Israelites, but also for their animals, servants (including slaves), and any foreigners living in Israel (Exodus 23:12; Deuteronomy 5:14-15).

The Sabbath reminds people of their special status as God's chosen people and that God is the creator of the word. Celebrating the Sabbath reminds people of their need for continual re-creation. [TLB, p. 927]

Dear Abner: For a long time now, I've been hearing that God keeps promises, but does God really care about what happens to me on any given day?
—Just Wondering

Dear Just Wondering: It's hard to imagine that the God who created heaven and earth cares about the details of one person's life. Well, let me assure you that God really does! Just as God cared whether the Israelites had enough to eat and drink, God cares about you! God says, "I am the Lord your God, and I will be there to help you wherever you go" (Joshua 1:5). Does that include times you spend with your family? With friends? At school? At play? You bet!

Campfire Talk

The Israelites thought that the ultimate test of survival meant they had to find food and water in the wilderness. Since God provided for those things, what was God really testing?

CLUES: Hebrews 11:1, 6.

Peter and Cornelius

Acts 10:1-48

Wild dreams and strange visions bring together two people from very different cultures. Their friends might have wondered ... YOU'RE FRIENDS WITH HIM?

30

In Caesarea there was a man named Cornelius, who was the captain of a group of [Roman] soldiers.... He had given a lot of money to the poor and was always praying to God. One afternoon at about 3 o'clock, Cornelius had a vision. He saw an angel from God ... calling him by name. Cornelius was surprised.... Then he asked, "What is this all about?"

The angel answered, "God has heard your prayers and knows about your gifts to the poor. Now send some men to Joppa for a man named Simon Peter. He is visiting with Simon the leather maker, who lives in a house near the sea." After saying this, the angel left. (verses 1-7, CEV)

Continued on page 32

Visions happen when God's Spirit or a messenger of God (such as an angel) speaks to the deepest thoughts of a person and provides a clear picture of something that person should do or say.

Continued from page 31

The next day about noon ... Peter went up on the roof of the house to pray and became very hungry.... He fell asleep and had a vision. He saw heaven open, and something came down like a huge sheet held up by its four corners. In it were all kinds of animals, snakes, and birds.

Peter said, "Lord, I've never eaten anything that is unclean and not fit to eat."

The voice spoke, "When God says that something can be used for food, don't say it isn't fit to eat."

This happened three times before the sheet was suddenly taken back to heaven.

(verses 9-12, 14-16, CEV)

Why would Peter pray on the roof of a house?

Many people living in Palestine in Jesus' day lived in one-room houses that sometimes included an area where animals were kept and fed. Roofs were flat and made of layers of branches packed with mud. Roofs were used for gardening and a place to sleep when it was hot. [TLB, p. 1818]

Illustration from TLB.

Purity— Clean and Unclean

Ancient Israel defined being *pure* in three ways: 1) to be free of dirt or pollution; 2) to have no contact with anything unfit for a religious person to touch; 3) to be free of actions that hurt others and go against God's commands.

According to the Law of Moses, different things could be clean or unclean (pure or impure). People could become unclean if they had certain kinds of diseases, when they touched a dead body, or when they ate certain foods, such as pork or some kinds of fish. The Law told the people what to avoid so they wouldn't become unclean. (See especially Leviticus 11-18.) It also told them how they could become clean again by waiting for a period of time and then being washed and making the right kind of sacrifice.

The early Christians understood that the sacrifice that made people pure and clean was the death of Jesus Christ (Mark 10:45). Jesus' blood was poured out for the forgiveness of sins (Matthew 26:28), and it cleanses his people from all sin (1 John 1:7). [TLB, p. 2031]

Peter was still wondering what all of this meant when the men sent by Cornelius came and stood at the gate. They had found their way to Simon's house and were asking if Simon Peter was staying there.

While Peter was still thinking about the vision, the Holy Spirit said to him, "Three men are here looking for you. Hurry down and go with them. Don't worry, I sent them." (verses 17-19, CEV)

Continued on page 34

The next morning, Peter and some of the Lord's followers in Joppa left with the men who had come from Cornelius.

Peter said to Cornelius, "I agreed to come here, but I want to know why you sent for me. Cornelius answered:

"Four days ago at about 3 o'clock in the afternoon I was praying at home. Suddenly a man in bright clothes stood in front of me. He said, 'Cornelius, God has heard your prayers, and he knows about your gifts to the poor. Now send to Joppa for Simon Peter. He is visiting in the home of Simon the leather maker, who lives near the sea.'"

I sent for you right away and you have been good enough to come. All of us are here in the presence of the Lord God, so that we can hear what he has to say.

(verses 23, 29-33, CEV)

Continued on page 36

Key Verse

God is pleased with everyone who worships him and does right, no matter what nation they come from. (Acts 10:35, CEV)

Opinion

CORNELIUS'S COOK COMPLAINS

Do you know how many mouths I have had to feed lately? Ever since Cornelius became a Christian, he spends his days praying and praising God. Sure, Cornelius does his usual tasks, but he does them in a new way, full of laughter and kindness. I don't know what's gotten into him. We used to have this understanding: I fixed his food, and he left me alone. Now I'm cooking for a crowd, and Cornelius is talking to me like I'm a friend. What is up with that guy?

The latest is that Cornelius claims to have seen an angel. And now a well-known man named Peter is coming here to eat. From what I hear, people from where Peter lives have strict laws about food. But Cornelius tells me not to worry about what to cook. Since the boss says not to worry, I'll just make the Roman specialty dishes his family prefers.

After everyone's done eating, I'm going ask someone about this Jesus Christ that they keep talking about. It's him that has put me into this fix, changing everything and everybody around here!

—The Cook

Peter then said:

"Now I am certain that God treats all people alike. God is pleased with everyone who worships him and does right, no matter what nation they come from."

(verses 34-35, CEV)

Gentiles

The English word *Gentile* comes from the Latin word for "people." In the Bible, Gentiles are all people who were not Jews. The descendants of Noah spread out over the world and became many nations and people (Genesis 10). God divided these nations by giving them different languages, because they had acted in evil ways (Genesis 11). But then God chose Abraham and Sarah and told them that he would use them and their descendants to bring God's blessing to "all the families of the earth" (Genesis 12:1-3).

In the New Testament, Simeon blessed the child Jesus and said that he will be a "light to the nations" (Luke 2:29-32). Jesus reached out to heal people who were not Jewish, like the man with the demon (Mark 5), the deaf man (Mark 7:31-37), and the servant of a Roman officer (Matthew 8:5-13).

Both Jews and Gentiles who trust what God has done through Jesus are accepted into the life of his new people (Galatians 2:11-16). Jesus died for the sins of the world, making it possible for everyone to share in God's kingdom. (Revelation 5:6-10). [TLB, p. 2033]

Dear Abner: Sometimes God seems so far away. I wish God and I could talk in person. How do I get in touch with God?—Good Buddy

Dear Good Buddy: The truth is, God is not as far away as you might think! And you can talk to God directly! Here's how it works. You don't need a satellite or telephone or any special equipment. All you need is a heart that wants to know God—and it sounds to me like you already have this! You can speak to God aloud or silently in your thoughts. You can even write God a letter. (There's no need to mail it; God knows what you've written.) God is eager to hear your prayers and looks forward to hearing from you.

Listening is important, too. God will communicate to you in many ways. Read the Bible to learn about God's plan for you. (Start with Jeremiah 29:11.) Worship with other Christians, and listen for God's word. God may even speak to you through the wisdom of other people. Just keep your heart and mind open, and you'll be surprised at all that God has to say!

Campfire Talk

People may have wondered why Peter and Cornelius were friends, but their love for Jesus is what brought them together. Read what God has to say about friendship in John 15:12-17; Colossians 3:12-14; 1 John 4:9-11.

Elijah and the Widow

1 Kings 17

A starving woman and her son invite a famous stranger to share their last meal. All the while they wonder how can he save them when … THERE'S NOTHING TO EAT!

Elijah was a prophet. One day he went to King Ahab and said, "I'm a servant of the living Lord, the God of Israel. And I swear in his name that it won't rain until I say so. There won't even be any dew on the ground." (verse 1, CEV) Continued on page 40

In Elijah's day, many people in the northern kingdom worshiped foreign gods, such as Baal and Asherah. The worship of these gods was encouraged by Israel's King Ahab and Queen Jezebel (1 Kings 16:30-33; 21:25-29). At that time, Elijah seems to have been the only prophet who had the courage to challenge the influence of powerful people.
[TLB, p. 1705]

Who's in Charge?

The drought will punish the people for their wickedness and demonstrate that Lord God, not Baal, is in control of the rains.
[TLB, p. 653]

Continued from page 39

Later, the Lord said to Elijah, "Leave and go across the Jordan River so you can hide near Cherith Creek. You can drink water from the creek and eat the food I've told the ravens to bring you."

Elijah obeyed the Lord and went to live near Cherith Creek. Ravens brought him bread and meat twice a day, and he drank water from the creek. But after a while, it dried up because there was no rain. (verses 2-7, CEV)

Who Are Today's Prophets?

Prophets are not always very popular, especially when, like Elijah, they call sinful people to obedience. (No one likes to be told, "Your behavior displeases God.") The drought that Elijah predicted proved that the God of Israel was all-powerful.

People began to take notice of what Elijah said. They recognized that God worked through Elijah to perform miracles and tell about the future.

The call to faithfulness and the expectation of God's will for the future is one hallmark of a prophet. Can you think of anyone today or in recent history who has spoken with a prophetic voice? Someone whose vision for the future reflects God's desire for justice and peace?

Hear This!

A prophet was someone who spoke God's message to the people or to their rulers. Many Jews in later centuries thought that Elijah would return to prepare for the day of judgment or for the coming of the Messiah. Read more about it in Malachi 4:1-6; Matthew 17:10-11; Mark 9:11-12. [TLB, p. 653]

BREAKING ALL THE RULES

Things were sure different back in Elijah's day! A man never spoke to a woman he did not know, especially a woman who was not an Israelite. Women had very little status in society. A woman whose husband died was doomed to a life of poverty. The widow of Zarephath did the best she could, but she knew there was little hope for her and her son.

Elijah defied many customs and traditions when he spoke to this woman. What could he have been thinking?

✓ The woman was walking alone, and Elijah was a stranger to her.

✓ She was not Jewish. (Read more about Gentiles on page 36.)

✓ As a widow, she had no man to protect and provide for her family.

✓ Despite the woman's poverty, Elijah dared to ask her for food!

Elijah believed and trusted in God's plan. He was more interested in obeying God than in keeping the cultural rules of the day. Jesus teaches us to care for people who need help. How is life today different from life in Elijah's day? How are things the same?

The Lord told Elijah, "Go to the town of Zarephath in Sidon and live there. I've told a widow in that town to give you food."

When Elijah came near the town gate of Zarephath, he saw a widow gathering sticks for a fire. "Would you please bring me a cup of water?" he asked. As she left to get the water, Elijah asked, "Would you also please bring me a piece of bread?"

(verses 8-11, CEV)    Continued on page 42

The widow answered, "In the name of the living Lord your God, I swear I don't have any bread. All I have is a handful of flour and a little olive oil. I'm on my way home now with these few sticks to cook what I have for my son and me. After that, we will starve to death."

Elijah said, "Everything will be fine. Do what you said. Go home and fix something for you and your son. But first, please make a small piece of bread and bring it to me. The Lord God of Israel has promised that your jar of flour won't run out and your bottle of oil won't dry up before he sends rain for the crops." (verses 12-14, CEV)

Key Verse

The LORD God of Israel has promised that your jar of flour won't run out and your bottle of oil won't dry up … (1 Kings 17:14, CEV)

God provides food for hungry people in other Bible stories. Find two of these stories in Mark 6:30-44; Exodus 15:22—16:36.

Opinion
LISTEN UP!

The prophet Elijah claims that the God of Israel is the only true God. Not only is Elijah bold enough to speak out against Baal, the Canaanite god, but he accuses Israel's King Ahab and Queen Jezebel of killing a man just to take his land and vineyard. King Ahab could have Elijah's head for saying such things!

Recently on Mt. Carmel, Elijah challenged Baal's priests to see whose god was stronger (1 Kings 16:29—19:18). Elijah called fire from heaven, which devoured the altar and pretty much proved his point.

Elijah is demanding that people turn back to the God of Israel. It might be wise to listen. Elijah obviously has the power of God behind him. He predicted a drought (1 Kings 17:1), provided food that didn't run out (1 Kings 17:14), and brought a dead boy back to life (1 Kings 17:17-24). How much more convincing do we need?

—A Concerned Citizen

The widow went home and did exactly what Elijah had told her. She and Elijah and her family had enough food for a long time. The Lord kept the promise that the prophet Elijah had made, and the woman did not run out of flour or oil.

(verses 15-16, CEV)

Marvelous Makeover

The outward things we can do to make ourselves look good makes little difference to how we feel inside. What really matters is whether or not we have hope and joy. The widow of Zarephath discovered the source of true hope and joy when she learned to trust God.

Before

Not knowing or trusting in God results in:
- fear
- loneliness
- worry
- despair

After

Knowing and trusting God for all our needs, both physical and spiritual, results in:
- love
- happiness
- peacefulness
- patience
- kindness
- goodness
- faithfulness
- gentleness
- self-control

Trusting in God does NOT mean that life will always be easy. It DOES mean that God is with us and gives us guidance and comfort. Above all, we have hope for the future—assurance of our salvation through Jesus! Read more about the fruits of the Spirit in Galatians 5:22.

Ask Abner

Dear Abner: My neighbor really seems to be struggling. He lost his job and has two little kids to care for. God provided for the widow of Zarephath, but how can I be sure that God will care for my neighbor?—The Boy Next Door

Dear Boy Next Door: It was good of you to notice and care about someone else's troubles! One of the important ways that God works is through the love and care of other people. Just as God provided for the widow through Elijah, God may provide for your neighbor through someone he knows. You can start by praying for your neighbor. Then be willing to be the instrument through which God will work. Use your imagination! Maybe your neighbor could use some help watching his children. Maybe your family could invite your neighbor's family over for dinner. Or maybe your neighbor just needs someone to talk to. Whatever you decide, talk to your parents first—and give thanks for all the ways that God provides!

Campfire Talk

Have you ever run out of something just when you needed it most? Have you ever run out of time, patience, or energy? What can we do in moments like these? In what ways is God there to help?

The widow must have been amazed that her flour and oil did not run out. But later, when her son became ill and died, all the flour and oil in the world would not bring him back to life.

Read about what happened next in 1 Kings 17:17-24.

How God Uses Miracles

God works miracles for many reasons. What miracles have you seen or experienced in your own life? What reasons do you think God had for those miracles? Read more about how God uses miracles.

Miracle	Scripture Passages
God saves or delivers people from trouble.	Exodus 14 Daniel 3:6 Act 12:6-12; 16:16-34
God provides food and other blessings.	Exodus 16:1—17:7 2 Kings 4:1-7 Luke 5:1-11 John 6:5-15; 21:1-14
God's purposes and glory are revealed.	Isaiah 6 Ezekiel 1 Zechariah 1:7—5:11 Acts 9:1-19; 10:1-48
God overcomes death.	2 Kings 4:18-37 Matthew 28:1-7 Luke 7:11-17 John 11:1-44 Acts 9:36-43

[TLB, p. 1726]

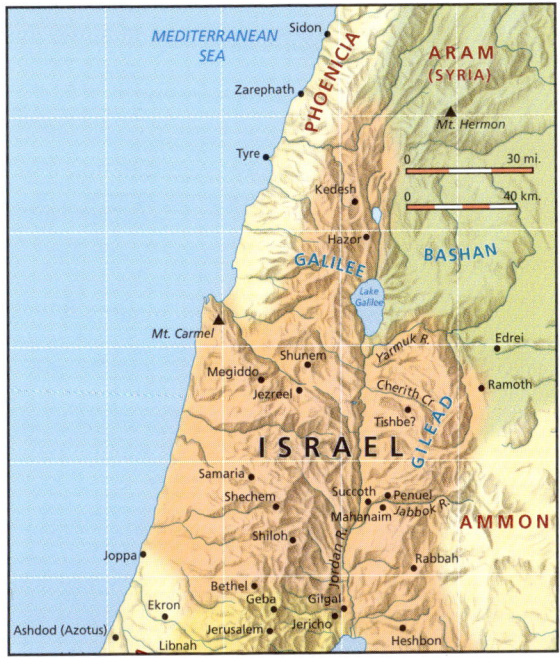

Find where King Ahab lived, in Samaria.

Read I Kings 18 and then find Mt. Carmel.

Find Zarephath.

Find Cherith Creek.

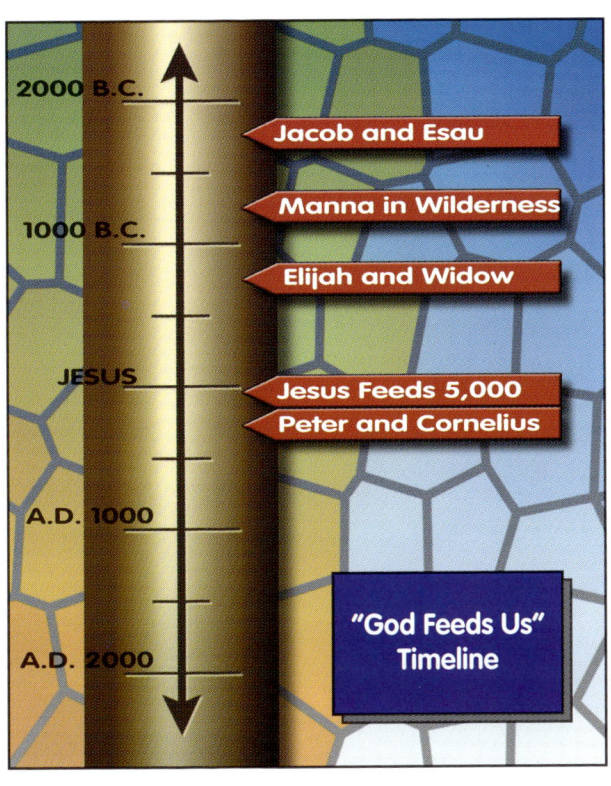

"God Feeds Us" Timeline